The Planet Promise
I promise to:

Rethink what I use and buy.
Refuse what I don't need.
Reduce my waste and carbon footprint.
Reuse things when I can.
Recycle as much as I can.
Rot food in a <u>compost bin</u>.
Repair broken things.

Earth's Eco-Warriors are starting a war on waste! But what is waste? Waste is all the things that we don't want or need. This can be the trash you throw away or clothes that don't fit you anymore. We all make waste, but waste is bad for the <u>environment</u>. We need to think about the ways we can reduce waste and how we can recycle the waste that we make.

www.littlebluehousebooks.com

Copyright © 2025 by Little Blue House, Mendota Heights, MN 55120. All rights reserved. No part of this book may be reproduced or utilized in any form or by any means without written permission from the publisher.

Little Blue House is distributed by North Star Editors: sales@northstareditions.com | 888-417-0195

Library of Congress Control Number: 2024936700

ISBN
979-8-89359-002-9 (hardcover)
979-8-89359-012-8 (paperback)
979-8-89359-032-6 (ebook pdf)
979-8-89359-022-7 (hosted ebook)

Printed in the United States of America
Mankato, MN
082024

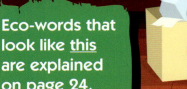

Eco-words that look like <u>this</u> are explained on page 24.

WE ARE EARTH'S ECO-WARRIORS

Are you an Eco-Warrior? Greta, Bailey, and Pietro are Earth's Eco-Warriors! Eco-Warriors care about the environment. They made the Planet Promise and are trying to save planet Earth.

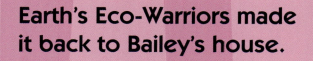

That evening, Bailey sorted through all her toys. She found lots of things she no longer played with. She packed them carefully into a box, ready for tomorrow's trip to the charity shop.

ALWAYS TRY TO REMEMBER THE PLANET PROMISE AND THINK OF ALL THE WAYS YOU COULD HELP THE ENVIRONMENT!

Being one of Earth's Eco-Warriors is tough work, but everybody has to do their part to help the planet. Is there anything you could donate?

REUSING PLASTIC BOTTLES

Would you like to be one of Earth's Eco-Warriors? Let's reuse a plastic bottle.

Plastic bottles can be reused and made into plant pots! Reusing things is an important part of the Planet Promise because it can help us reduce our waste.

THINGS YOU WILL NEED

- Sticky tape
- Scissors
- Twine or string to decorate
- Soil
- Two-liter plastic bottle
- A small plant or flower

1. Remove the label and lid from the bottle, and ask an adult to cut the bottle in half. Leave room for the plant's roots to grow.

ASK AN ADULT FOR HELP WITH THE SCISSORS. AN INJURED ECO-WARRIOR IS A SAD ECO-WARRIOR!

2. Cover the sharp edge of the bottle with sticky tape.

3. Put soil into the pot until it is about 1.5 inches (4 cm) high.

4. Gently hold the plant in the pot. Cover the plant's roots with soil.

5. Press the soil so the plant is snug.

6. Decorate your new pot with twine or string.

DON'T FORGET TO WASH AND RECYCLE THE PLASTIC BOTTLE WHEN THE PLANT IS TOO BIG FOR IT.

ECO-WORDS

compost bin	A special bin where yard waste and some food scraps turn into soil.
decompose	When something breaks down or rots.
donate	To give something away to help a cause, such as a charity.
energy	A type of power, such as light or heat, that can be used to do something.
environment	The natural world.
harmful gases	Things that get into the air and are bad for the environment.
incinerator	A machine that burns waste.
landfill	Where waste is buried.
processes	Sets of steps that happen in an order to get something done.
recycling plant	A building where waste is recycled.
single-use plastic	Something that is made from plastic and meant to be used once, such as a plastic bag or water bottle.
toxins	Dangerous and harmful things.

INDEX

clothes, 2, 4–8, 10, 18–19
environment, 2–3, 5, 10, 21
landfill, 4–5, 7, 10, 14, 16
litter, 10, 12, 18
Planet Promise, 2–3, 12, 21–22
recycling, 2, 11, 13–18, 23
single-use plastics, 10
toys, 8–9, 19–20
waste, 2–3, 6, 11, 13–16, 22

PHOTO CREDITS

Cover & Throughout – Olga1818, N.MacTavish, Satika, Nadya_Art, Squishy Doom, NotionPic, 2&3 – Elegant Solution, Naddya, AQmari, rok77, Oceloti, SunshineVector, Olly Molly, Alena Nv, Elena Sapronova, 6&7 – Graf Vishenka, IMissisHope, MicroOne, Mascha Tace, 8&9 – mutsuMaks, Iconic Bestiary, BlueRing Media, 10&11 – StockSmartStart, Lemberg Vector studio, billedfab, DeawSS, Vectors Bang, 12&13 – Roi and Roi, 14&15 – Mironova Iuliia, DRogatnev, BlueRingMedia, 16&17 – Dukesn, BigMouse, Terdpong, 20&21 – Pogorelova Olga, 22&23 – Irina Skokova, grmarc, Marina Akinina, Sanju Graphic Artist, belander, Volosovich Igor.

Images are courtesy of Shutterstock.com. With thanks to Getty Images, Thinkstock Photo, and iStockphoto.

All facts, statistics, web addresses, and URLs in this book were verified as valid and accurate at the time of writing. No responsibility for any changes to external websites or references can be accepted by either the author or the publisher.